Unforgettable
Edible Bible Crafts

NANCY I. SANDERS and NANETTE WILLIAMS

Illustrated by BECKY RADTKE

Scripture taken from the HOLY BIBLE, NEW INTERNATIONAL VERSION®. NIV®. Copyright © 1973, 1978, 1984 by International Bible Society. Used by permission of Zondervan Publishing House. All rights reserved.

Copyright © 1999 Concordia Publishing House
3558 S. Jefferson Avenue, St. Louis, MO 63118-3968
Manufactured in the United States of America

Teachers who purchase this product may reproduce pages for classroom use. Parents and other individuals who purchase this product may reproduce pages as needed for in-home completion of activities.

All rights reserved. Except as noted above, no part of this publication may be reproduced, stored in a retrieval system, or transmitted, in any form or by any means, electronic, mechanical, photocopying, recording, or otherwise, without the prior written permission of Concordia Publishing House.

2 3 4 5 6 7 8 9 10   08 07 06 05 04 03 02 01 00

CONTENTS

Creation Pudding (Genesis 1:25) - - - - - - - - - - - - - - - - 6

Bite the Apple! (Acts 5:31) - - - - - - - - - - - - - - - - - - 7

Noah's Animal Cupcakes (Genesis 6:20) - - - - - - - - - - - - 8

Noah's Ark Hats (Genesis 8:1) - - - - - - - - - - - - - - - - - 9

Balloon Clown (Genesis 21:6) - - - - - - - - - - - - - - - - - 10

Rebekah's Necklace (Genesis 24:53) - - - - - - - - - - - - - 11

Jacob's Present (Genesis 33:11) - - - - - - - - - - - - - - - 12

Bee Basket (Numbers 13:27) - - - - - - - - - - - - - - - - - 13

Trumpet of Jericho (Joshua 6:20) - - - - - - - - - - - - - - 14

Mother's Day Gift (Ruth 1:16) - - - - - - - - - - - - - - - - 15

Friendship Games (1 Samuel 18:3) - - - - - - - - - - - - - - 16

Celebration Rosettes (2 Samuel 6:15) - - - - - - - - - - - - 18

Stained-Glass Cookies (1 Kings 5:5) - - - - - - - - - - - - - 19

The Queen of Sheba's Scepter (1 Kings 10:9) - - - - - - - - 20

King Solomon's Scepter (1 Kings 8:15) - - - - - - - - - - - 21

Praise Drum and Tambourine (2 Chronicles 7:6a) - - - - - - 22

Nehemiah's Dominoes (Nehemiah 2:20a) - - - - - - - - - - 24

Queen Esther's Crown (Esther 4:14) - - - - - - - - - - - - - 25

Elephant Toss (Job 40:15a) - - - - - - - - - - - - - - - - - 26

Shepherd Name Card (Psalm 23:1) - - - - - - - - - - - - - - 27

King David's Crown (Psalm 34:8) - - - - - - - - - - - - - - - 28

Marshmallow Spear (Psalm 119:103) - - - - - - - - - - - - - 29

Uniquely You Accessory (Psalm 139:1–2) - - - - - - - - - - 30

Bow of Beauty (Proverbs 31:30) - - - - - - - - - - - - - - - 31

Happiness Necklaces (Ecclesiastes 3:4) - - - - - - - - - - - 32

Strawberry Flower Centerpiece (Song of Songs 2:12) - - - - 34

Star Glasses (Matthew 2:10) - - - - - - - - - - - - - - - - - 35

Decorated Spoon (Matthew 6:28) - - - - - - - - - - - - - - 36

Sheep Puppet Treats (Matthew 25:40) - - - - - - - - - - - 37

Chew-Chew Train (Mark 10:14) - - - - - - - - - - - - - - - 38

Welcome Wreath (Luke 7:44) - - - - - - - - - - - - - - - - 39

Birds' Nests (Luke 9:58) - - - - - - - - - - - - - - - - - - - 40

Mary and Martha Treats (Luke 10:41–42) - - - - - - - - - - 41

The Banquet's Garland (Luke 14:15) - - - - - - - - - - - - 42

Search for the Lost Coin (Luke 15:10) - - - - - - - - - - - 43

Picnic Games (John 6:14) - - - - - - - - - - - - - - - - - - 44

Dramatic Masks (John 11:25–26) - - - - - - - - - - - - - - 46

The Servant's Sandals (John 13:15) - - - - - - - - - - - - 47

Resurrection Celebration (Luke 24:6a) - - - - - - - - - - - 48

Bingo Love! (1 Corinthians 13:13) - - - - - - - - - - - - - 49

Fruit of the Spirit Bracelet (Galatians 5:22–23) - - - - - - 50

Anchor of Hope Balloon (Hebrews 6:19) - - - - - - - - - - 51

Party Decorations to Eat

- Bee Basket
- Celebration Rosettes
- Shepherd Name Card
- Strawberry Flower Centerpiece
- Decorated Spoon
- Sheep Puppet Treats
- Welcome Wreath
- The Banquet's Garland
- Anchor of Hope Balloon

Edible Toys

- Balloon Clown
- Trumpet of Jericho
- Praise Drum and Tambourine
- Chew-Chew Train
- Resurrection Celebration

Unforgettable Gifts to Give and Eat

- Jacob's Present
- Mother's Day Gift
- Mary and Martha Treats
- The Servant's Sandals

Decorate and Eat!

- Creation Pudding
- Noah's Animal Cupcakes
- Stained-Glass Cookies
- Marshmallow Spear
- Birds' Nests

Edible Games

- Bite the Apple!
- Friendship Games
  - *Tic-Tac-Toe*
  - *Catch-It Cone*
  - *Pick-up Sticks*
- Nehemiah's Dominoes
- Elephant Toss
- Search for the Lost Coin
- Picnic Games
  - *Bubble Gum Contest*
  - *Waffle Cone Toss*
  - *Marshmallow Tag*
- Bingo Love!

Costumes to Nibble and Wear

- Noah's Ark Hats
- Rebekah's Necklace
- The Queen of Sheba's Scepter
- King Solomon's Scepter
- Queen Esther's Crown
- King David's Crown
- Uniquely You Accessory
- Bow of Beauty
- Happiness Necklaces
  - *Shiny Necklace*
  - *Scrumptious Necklace*
- Star Glasses
- Dramatic Masks
- Fruit of the Spirit Bracelet

(These symbols are used throughout this book to help you reference the type of each activity.)

*Dedicated to Rachael and Lauren and all
the children I've ever done parties for.
Love, Shimmer the clown.*

*To Micah, with fond memories of the unforgettable
visit we had with you at Christmas. You're always
welcome to come see us in sunny California!
With love from your Aunt Nancy.*

UNFORGETTABLE EDIBLE BIBLE CRAFTS

Creation Pudding

In the very beginning, God created the whole world. He even made the dirt and the wiggly, squiggly worms. God made everything!

Bible Verse

God made ... all the creatures that move along the ground according to their kinds. And God saw that it was good.
Genesis 1:25

Materials Needed

Individual cups of ready-to-eat chocolate pudding
Chocolate wafer cookies
Gummed candy in the shape of worms

Tools to Use

Rolling pin, if needed

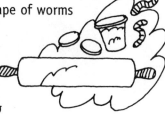

Making the Creation Pudding

1. Crumble the chocolate wafers into fine crumbs, using the rolling pin if needed.
2. Open the package of pudding and sprinkle the cookie crumbs over the top.
3. Stick in several gummed worms for a fun-filled treat.

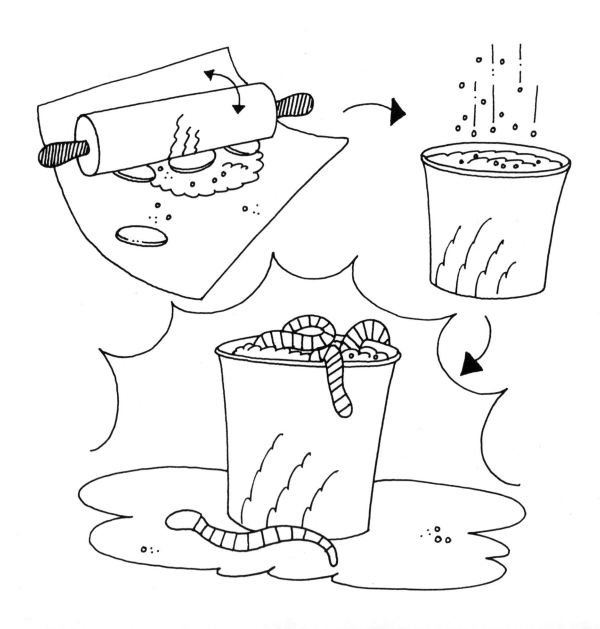

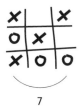

Bite the Apple!

When Adam and Eve ate the fruit of the tree of knowledge of good and evil, they disobeyed God and sin entered the world. However, God designed a plan for salvation by sending His Son, Jesus, to take the punishment for our sins on the cross.

Bible Verse

God exalted Him to His own right hand as Prince and Savior that He might give repentance and forgiveness of sins to Israel. Acts 5:31

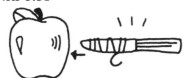

Materials Needed

Firm apples
String

Tools to Use

Table knife (not sharp)
Stopwatch

Playing the Game and Making the Apples

1. Wash and dry the apples.
2. Wrap the end of the string over the tip of the knife, and use the knife to poke the string through the center of the apple.
3. Tie the apples shoulder-high from a swing set or set of monkey bars. Space the apples two feet apart from each other.
4. To play the game, divide the children into pairs. One partner must block the apple with his shoulder to keep it from swinging while the other partner takes one bite from the apple. Have them switch and repeat this step until their apple contains two bites. The pair who finishes in the shortest time wins.

Noah's Animal Cupcakes

God brought the animals to the ark so Noah could care for them. Use these cupcakes as a centerpiece by arranging them in pairs along the length of your table.

Bible Verse

Two of every kind of bird, of every kind of animal and of every kind of creature that moves along the ground will come to you to be kept alive.
Genesis 6:20

Materials Needed

Cupcakes
Prepared frosting
Cookies in the shape of animals

Tools to Use

Plastic knives

Decorating the Cupcakes

1. Use the plastic knives to frost the cupcakes.
2. Stand one animal cookie on top of each cupcake.
3. Find matching pairs of animals and arrange them along the table as if they are marching into the ark. Include a toy ark in the centerpiece, if desired.

Noah's Ark Hats

God cared for Noah and the animals. He also loves and cares for each of us.

Bible Verse

But God remembered Noah and all the wild animals and the livestock that were with him in the ark. Genesis 8:1

Materials Needed

Cardboard party hats in solid colors
Variety of individually wrapped candy, such as:
  hard candy
  peppermints
  jaw breakers
  sticks of gum
Lightweight poster board
Cookie sprinkles
Animal-shaped cookie cutters

Tools to Use

Glue stick
Scissors
Pencil

Decorating the Noah's Ark Hats

1. Randomly glue the wrapped candy around the purchased hat.
2. Use a cookie cutter to trace an animal shape on the poster board. Cut out the shape.
3. Spread glue on the front of the shape and decorate with cookie sprinkles.
4. Glue the shape to the top of the hat.
5. Make a parade and march around the room, pretending to be an animal on the way to Noah's ark!

Balloon Clown

When Abraham and Sarah were old, God gave them the son they'd been wanting for many years. They named him Isaac and he brought laughter into their lives. As we make this silly clown and laugh at how funny it looks, let's thank God for the good things He brings to our lives.

Bible Verse

Sarah said, "God has brought me laughter, and everyone who hears about this will laugh with me." Genesis 21:6

Materials Needed

Duplicated patterns on page 52
9-inch balloon
Ribbon suitable for curling
Variety of small, wrapped candy
Small, unwrapped candy pieces
Poster board
Typing paper

Tools to Use

Glue stick
Craft glue
Scissors
Clear tape
Crayons and markers

Making the Balloon Clown

1. Cut out the pattern for the clown's feet and glue this to a piece of poster board. Cut out the poster board feet.
2. Decorate the feet by gluing candy on the poster board in fun designs. Small pieces can be glued on for toenails.
3. Inflate the balloon. Tie a big knot in the balloon. Push the knot through the hole on the feet and tape the knot underneath the poster board.
4. Stand the balloon up to decorate the face. Choose the eyes, nose, and mouth you want to use from the provided patterns, or make you own. Color these and glue them to the balloon.
5. Curl strands of ribbon and glue these to the clown for hair.
6. Now join in laughter with your friends as you look at each other's clowns and praise God for the good things He brings to our lives.

Rebekah's Necklace

Abraham's servant prayed for God to find a wife for Isaac. God led the servant to Rebekah and the servant thanked the Lord for His help.

Bible Verse

Then the servant brought out gold and silver jewelry and articles of clothing and gave them to Rebekah; he also gave costly gifts to her brother and to her mother.
Genesis 24:53

Materials Needed

Gummed candy
Hard circle candies with holes, such as Lifesavers
Colorful plastic straws

Tools to Use

Floss
Embroidery needle
Scissors

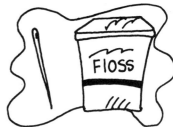

Creating Rebekah's Necklace

1. Using three feet of floss, thread the needle and poke it through a gummed candy. Tie a knot around the candy, leaving an 8-inch tail of floss.
2. Cut the straws into 1-inch and 2-inch lengths. Thread an assortment of straws and candies on the necklace, always putting a gummed candy on each end of each straw to prevent them from sliding too freely.
3. When the necklace is finished, tie a knot around the last gummed candy, leaving an 8-inch tail of floss.
4. To wear the necklace, tie the tails of floss together.

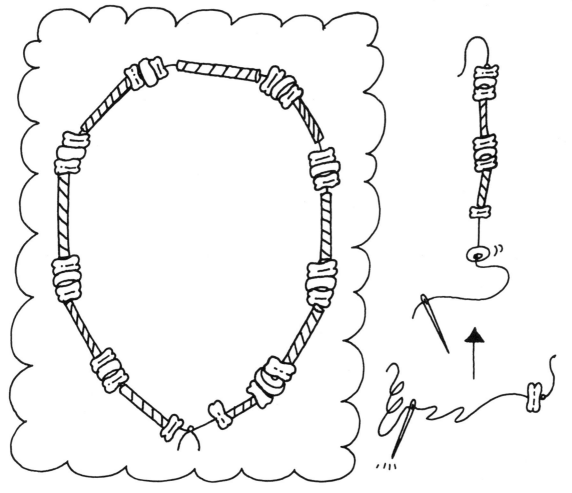

Jacob's Present

When Jacob returned to his homeland he gave his brother, Esau, a present.

Bible Verse

Please accept the present that was brought to you, for God has been gracious to me and I have all I need.
Genesis 33:11

Materials Needed

Six graham cracker squares, per project
Bubble-gum tape
Ready-to-use frosting
1" piece of candy such as bon bons
½-inch round candy, such as Milkduds or Junior Mints
Paper plate

Tool to Use

Plastic knife

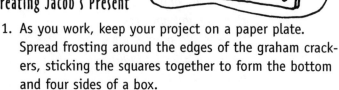

Creating Jacob's Present

1. As you work, keep your project on a paper plate. Spread frosting around the edges of the graham crackers, sticking the squares together to form the bottom and four sides of a box.
2. Carefully place the 1" piece of candy inside the box.
3. Use frosting to attach a graham cracker to the top of the box.
4. Following the illustration as a guide, use frosting to stick pieces of bubble-gum tape up two sides of the box and across the top. Stick a second piece of bubble-gum tape on the opposite sides and across the top, making the box look like a wrapped present.
5. To make the bow, fold a 4-inch piece of bubble-gum tape in half. Repeat with a second piece and place both pieces in the shape of an X on the top of the present. Use frosting to stick a ½-inch piece of candy in the center.

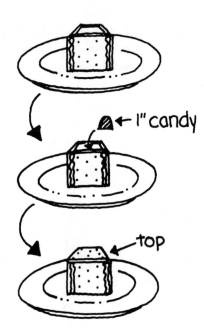

Bee Basket

When God freed the Israelites from slavery, He promised to lead them to a land flowing with milk and honey. Honey is made by bees and is very sweet. As we eat the treats found in this basket, we can remember the sweet promises God makes to us.

Bible Verse

They gave Moses this account: "We went into the land to which you sent us, and it does flow with milk and honey! Here is its fruit."
Numbers 13:27

Materials Needed

Duplicated pattern from page 53
Assorted mints

Tools to Use

Scissors
Crayons or markers

Making the Bee Basket

1. Cut out the pattern for the basket and color.
2. Fold the bees up from the base and join their wings at the slits to form the basket.
3. Fill the basket with mints, and put one at each person's place setting.

Trumpet of Jericho

When God brought the Israelites into the Promised Land, they did not win their first battle by fighting. God instructed them to march around the city of Jericho blowing their trumpets. After the Israelites obeyed God's commands, the walls of Jericho came crashing down.

Bible Verse

When the trumpets sounded, the people shouted, and at the sound of the trumpet, when the people gave a loud shout, the wall collapsed; so every man charged straight in, and they took the city.
Joshua 6:20

Materials Needed

Short cardboard tube, such as one from toilet paper
Gift wrap
Ribbon suitable for curling
Waxed paper
Rubber bands
Assortment of wrapped candy

Tools to Use

Scissors
Glue

Making the Trumpet of Jericho

1. Cut a 4½" x 7" piece of gift wrap. Glue this around the outside of the cardboard tube.
2. Cut two 4" circles from the waxed paper. Place one waxed paper circle over one end of the tube. Use a rubber band to hold it tightly in place.
3. Put several pieces of candy inside the tube.
4. Cover the other end of the tube in the same manner as the first. Decorate the tube by attaching curling ribbon to the rubber bands.
5. To play your trumpet, open one end of the tube and eat the candy. Hum into this open end and hear your trumpet sound!

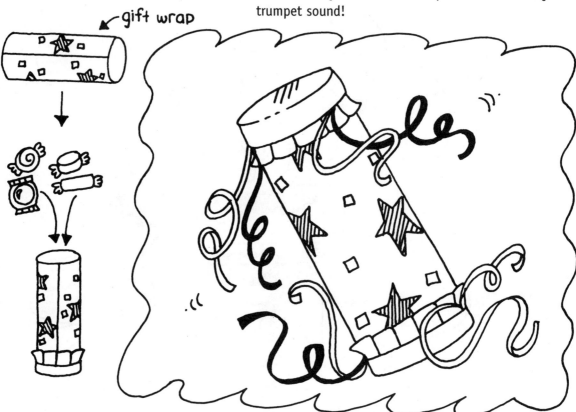

Mother's Day Gift

Ruth loved her mother-in-law, Naomi. Ruth promised to follow Naomi home to Bethlehem and love Naomi's God. As children, we can show our love and appreciation for our own mothers by giving them this gift on their special day.

Bible Verse

But Ruth replied, "Don't urge me to leave you or to turn back from you. Where you go I will go, and where you stay I will stay. Your people will be my people and your God my God." Ruth 1:16

Materials Needed

Chocolate suitable for melting
Plastic spoon
Silver spoon, optional
Plastic wrap
½-inch wide ribbon

Tools to Use

Cooking utensils

Making the Gift

1. Melt the chocolate in a microwave or on the stove.
2. When the chocolate is melted, allow it to cool and thicken slightly. Dip the rounded part of the spoon into the chocolate. (Optional: Find an old silver spoon at a thrift store to coat with chocolate as a truly elegant gift!)
3. Wrap the chocolate end of the spoon in plastic wrap. Use a ribbon to tie the plastic bag closed at the base of the spoon. This spoon may be used to stir a warm drink.

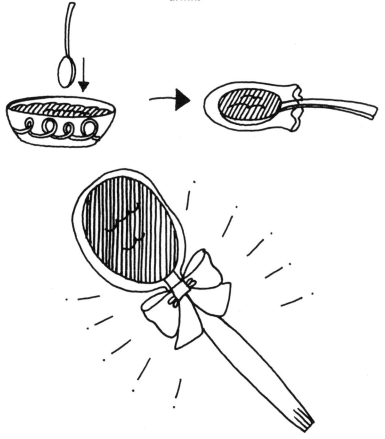

Friendship Games

David and Jonathan were friends. They enjoyed spending time together. With these games, you can spend time having fun with your friends too.

Bible Verse

And Jonathan made a covenant with David because he loved him as himself. 1 Samuel 18:3

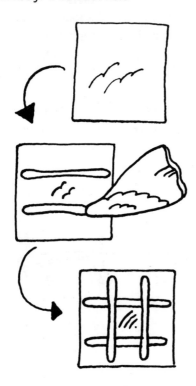

Tic-Tac-Toe

Materials Needed

Fruit leather
Premixed frosting
Two different colors of hard candy, 5 pieces of each color

Tools to Use

Plastic sandwich bag
Scissors

Making Tic-Tac-Toe

1. Cut the fruit leather into a 4" square. This makes the game board.
2. Use the scissors to snip off the corner of the sandwich bag. Fill the bag with 3 to 4 tablespoons of frosting.
3. Holding the bag in your hands, squeeze frosting out of the hole and onto the fruit leather game board. Make two horizontal lines and two vertical lines that cross over each other. This forms nine playing spaces. Follow the illustration as a guide.
4. Give each player one set of matching hard candy. Taking turns, each player places one candy in a space at a time. The first player who gets three candies in a row wins.
5. Repeat the game as often as you like, then gobble it up!

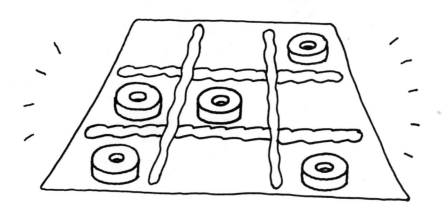

Catch-It Cone

Materials Needed
Ice-cream cone
Large marshmallow
Elastic string, available at fabric stores

Tools to Use
Embroidery needle

Making the Catch-It Cone
1. Use the needle to poke a hole near the open edge of the cone.
2. Thread the needle with a 2½' length of elastic string. Use the needle to thread the elastic string through the center of the marshmallow. Tie the string in a knot around the marshmallow.
3. Poke the other end of the string through the hole in the cone and tie into a knot.

Playing with the Catch-It Cone
1. Hold the cone in one hand.
2. Using a swinging motion, gently toss the marshmallow up into the air and try to catch it inside the cone.
3. Have a contest with your friend to see who catches the marshmallow most often!

Pick-Up Sticks

Materials Needed
Candy-filled straws, such as Pixie Sticks, in a variety of colors

Playing the Game
1. Number and assign points to each color straw. For instance, you can have one blue straw, five red straws, five green straws, and 10 purple straws. Here is a handy chart for points you earn for each straw:
   Blue—25 Points
   Red—10 Points Each
   Green—5 Points Each
   Purple—1 Point Each
2. Drop the straws in a pile. Take turns picking up the straws, one at a time. If you disturb another straw or make a straw wiggle that you were not trying to pick up, put the straw back and lose your turn.
3. After all the straws have been picked up, count your points. The player with the most points wins.
4. To give this game as a gift to a friend, tie the straws together with curling ribbon as shown. Duplicate the instructions, punch a hole in them, and attach the instructions with curling ribbon.

Celebration Rosettes

When King David brought the ark of the covenant home to Jerusalem, he rejoiced with all his might. After worshiping the Lord, the king gave each Israelite at the celebration some dates, raisins, and a loaf of bread to take home.

Bible Verse

[David] and the entire house of Israel brought up the ark of the LORD with shouts and the sound of trumpets.
2 Samuel 6:15

Materials Needed

Poster board
Long, narrow tubes of wrapped, hard candies
Miniature boxes of raisins
Ribbon suitable for looping
Peel-and-stick ribbon bows

Tools to Use

Tape
Glue
Scissors
Hole punch, double-sided tape, or stapler

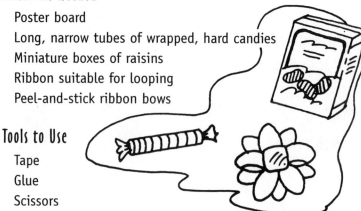

Making the Rosettes

1. Cut a 5" circle from poster board.
2. Cut a 6' length of ribbon. Double the ribbon over several times so loops of ribbon show all around the circle. When finished, tape the ribbon to the back of the poster board. Let the ends of ribbon hang down when the rosette is displayed.
3. On the front of the rosette, glue the miniature box of raisins in the center of the poster board circle. Use the illustration as a guide to glue the candies around the circle. Stick a bow on the raisin box.
4. Hang the rosette up using double-sided tape, or staple it to the wall. Or punch a hole in the top of the poster board circle, tie a ribbon loop on the rosette, and hang from a nail.

Stained-Glass Cookies

Solomon built the temple. It was very beautiful and was a special place to worship God. Our churches are special places where we go to worship God. Beautiful stained-glass windows remind us of the many reasons to praise God.

Bible Verse

"I intend, therefore, to build a temple for the Name of the LORD my God, as the LORD told my father David, when He said, `Your son whom I will put on the throne in your place will build the temple for My Name.'"
1 Kings 5:5

Materials Needed

Duplicated pattern from page 56
Favorite recipe for sugar cookie dough
Hard, round candies with holes, in a variety of colors
Nonstick cooking spray

Tools to Use

Baking pans and utensils
Rolling pin
Plastic knife

Making the Stained-Glass Cookies

1. Prepare the dough for the sugar cookies. Use the rolling pin to roll the dough out flat.
2. Place the pattern on the dough. Use the plastic knife to cut around the pattern. Cut the center area out.
3. Place these window cookies on a cookie sheet sprayed with nonstick cooking spray. Crush the hard candies with the rolling pin and place several pieces of crushed candy in the empty center of each window.
4. Bake the cookies. The candy will melt and give a stained-glass effect.

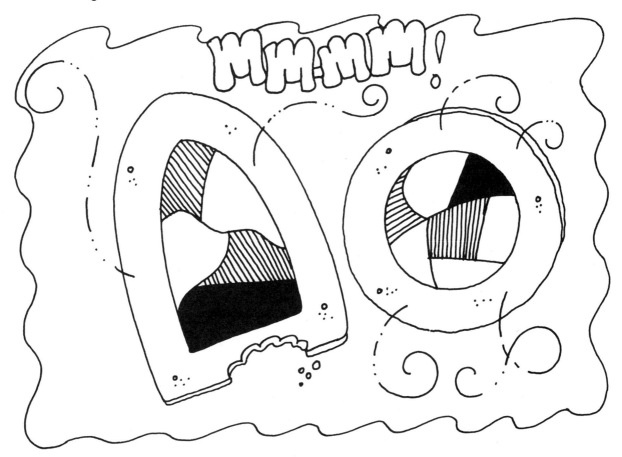

The Queen of Sheba's Scepter

The Queen of Sheba heard marvelous things about King Solomon. She traveled from far away to visit the king to see if all these things were true. After talking with King Solomon, the Queen of Sheba gave him a wonderful compliment and many beautiful gifts.

Bible Verse

Praise be to the LORD your God, who has delighted in you.
1 Kings 10:9

Materials Needed

A candy-filled straw
Tinsel-covered wire garland in 1' lengths
Ribbon suitable for curling and shredding
Variety of candy, individually wrapped

Tools to Use

Glue stick
Scissors
Ribbon shredder
Tape

Making the Queen of Sheba's Scepter

1. Lay the tinsel-covered wire garland flat on a work surface.
2. Use a 3' piece of ribbon to curl and shred. Repeat with another color.
3. Holding the ribbon together, loosely wrap the shredded ribbon along the length of the wire garland, leaving about a 2' tail of ribbon. Tie wrapped candies to the ends of the ribbon.
4. Hold the wire garland and the ribbon as one piece, forming a circle. Twist the two ends of the garland tightly together, leaving a 1" stem on the wire.
5. Tape the stem to the end of the candy-filled straw.
6. Hold up the scepter and give a compliment to someone!

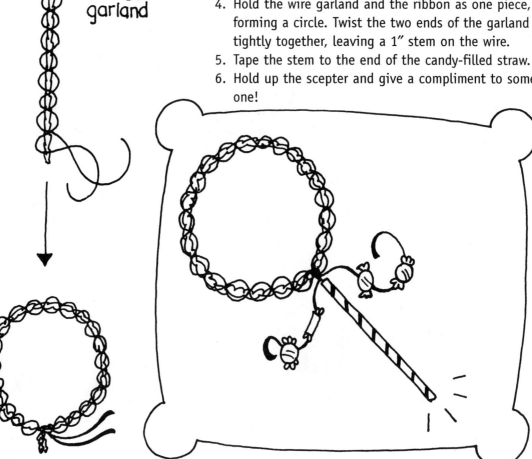

King Solomon's Scepter

After the temple was built, King Solomon said thank You to God. We, too, can thank God for the many things He does for us.

Bible Verse

Praise be to the LORD, the God of Israel, who with His own hand has fulfilled what He promised. 1 Kings 8:15

Materials Needed

2' long jumbo candy-filled straw
Large jawbreaker, about 3" in diameter
Clear cellophane wrap

Tools to Use

Scissors
Clear tape
Hot glue gun

Designing the Scepter

1. Cut off the end of the candy-filled straw and open the end about one inch.
2. Cut a square of cellophane large enough to cover the jawbreaker.
3. Wrap the jawbreaker in cellophane, trimming and taping as needed.
4. Use the hot glue gun to glue the jawbreaker to the top of the candy-filled straw, being careful to wedge the jawbreaker in tightly so the candy will not spill.
5. Hold the scepter and say thank You to God for something that He has done in your life.

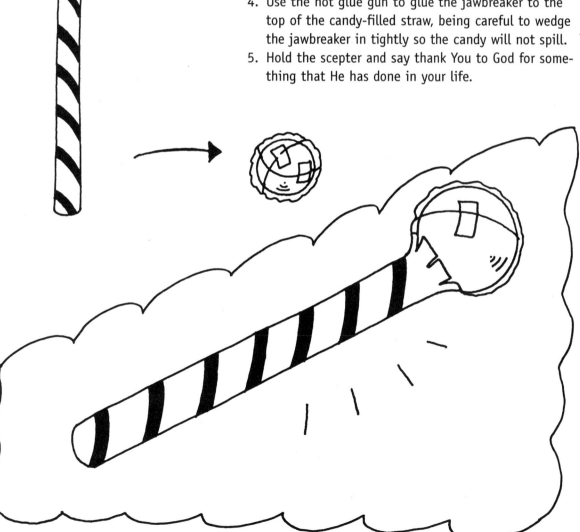

Praise Drum and Tambourine

Solomon dedicated the newly built temple to God. Everyone praised God and gave Him thanks through music and song.

Bible Verse

The priests took their positions, as did the Levites with the Lord's musical instruments, which King David had made for praising the Lord and which were used when he gave thanks, saying, "His love endures forever."
2 Chronicles 7:6a

Praise Drum

Materials Needed
Poster board
Gift wrap
Piece of fruit leather
Curling ribbon
Rubber band
Round lollipop with a candy-covered center

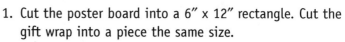

Tools to Use
Scissors
Glue stick
Clear, wide tape

Making the Praise Drum

1. Cut the poster board into a 6" x 12" rectangle. Cut the gift wrap into a piece the same size.
2. Glue the gift wrap to the poster board.
3. Roll the poster board into a cylinder with the gift wrap side facing outward and tape the edge, overlapping the edges ½ inch.
4. Cover the top of the cylinder with a square of fruit leather. Use a rubber band to hold it in place.
5. Tie a length of curling ribbon around the rubber band.
6. Play the drum gently with the round lollipop, and praise the Lord!

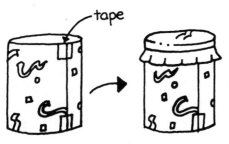

Tambourine

Materials Needed
Wooden embroidery hoop
Pieces of wrapped candy
Jingle bells
Narrow ribbon
1" wide ribbon

Tools to Use
Scissors
Glue

Making the Tambourine

1. Use one of the hoops to make one tambourine. (Note: An embroidery hoop set makes two tambourines.)
2. Spread glue one fourth of the way around the outside edge of the hoop. Wrap the wide ribbon around the hoop, gluing it in place. Add glue as you go, wrapping the ribbon around and around until the entire hoop is covered with the ribbon.
3. Use 10" lengths of narrow ribbon to tie the bells, one at a time, all around the tambourine.
4. Glue pieces of candy on the hoop and tie them with ribbon.
5. Shake your tambourine and rejoice!

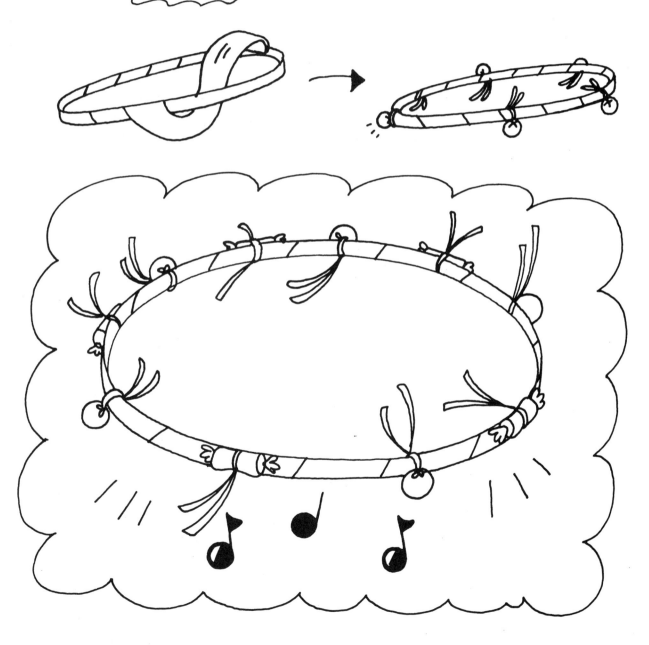

Nehemiah's Dominoes

Nehemiah followed God's call to return to Jerusalem and rebuild its damaged wall. As you play this game of dominoes, building one piece upon another, remember that God gives us strength to complete the work He calls us to do.

Bible Verse

I answered them by saying, "The God of heaven will give us success. We His servants will start rebuilding."
Nehemiah 2:20a

Materials Needed

Graham crackers
Ready-to-use colored frosting
Small hot cinnamon candy

Tools to Use

Plastic knife

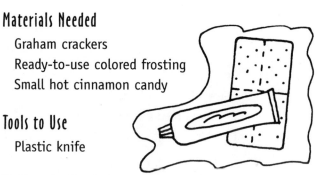

Making the Dominoes

1. Break the graham cracker into fourths to resemble dominoes.
2. Spread each square on the dominoes with frosting, staying away from the edges.
3. Put different amounts of small candies, from one to six, on each square of the dominoes.
4. When the dominoes are ready, play a game by dividing them in half. Place a cracker with a double six in the center. Players add dominoes by placing matching sides together. If the player does not have a matching domino, he or she passes. The first player to use all his or her dominoes wins the game.

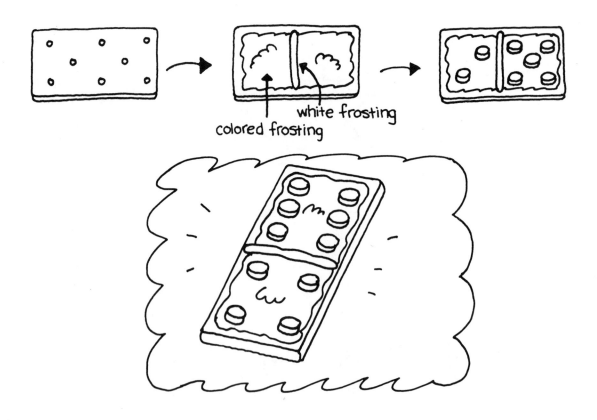

Queen Esther's Crown

Queen Esther faced a terrible situation. All the Jews, including herself, were to be killed. Because she courageously spoke to the king, a new law was made that protected the Jews from death. As you wear your crown, think about things God wants you to do that are difficult. Remember Queen Esther's example, and pray for courage to do what is best.

Bible Verse

And who knows but that you have come to your position for such a time as this? Esther 4:14

Materials Needed

Tinsel-covered wire garland
Ribbon suitable for curling and shredding
Metallic ribbon
Individually wrapped candy such as:
  peppermints
  hard candy

Tools to Use

Scissors
Ribbon shredder
Hole punch

Decorating the Crown

1. Measure each child's head and cut a piece of wire garland, adding one inch for tying the ends together.
2. Lay the wire garland out flat on a work surface.
3. Use a 4' piece of ribbon to curl and shred. Cut a 3' length of metallic ribbon.
4. Holding the ribbons together, loosely wrap the ribbon along the length of the wire garland, leaving about a 2' tail of ribbon.
5. Holding the wire garland and ribbon as one piece, form a circle and twist the two ends of the garland tightly together.
6. Punch a hole in the candy wrappers. Trimming some of the ribbon tails to a shorter length, tie the candy to the ends of the ribbon.

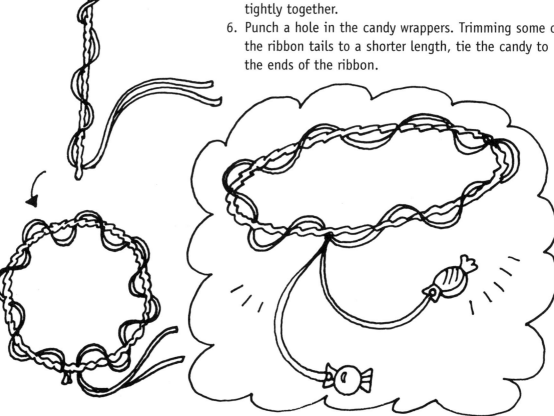

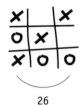

Elephant Toss

When Job was sick and covered with boils, he complained that God wasn't big enough to make him better. God reminded Job of the elephant and the other big animals He created. If God was bigger than an elephant, then God was bigger than everything! This showed Job that God was bigger than any problem there ever was. God was the only One who could really help Job.

Bible Verse

"Look at the behemoth, which I made along with you." Job 40:15a

Note: Behemoth can mean elephant, hippopotamus, dinosaur, or other very large land animal.

Materials Needed

Duplicated pattern on pages 54-55
Gray construction paper
Large coffee can
Peanuts in their shell

Tools to Use

Crayons and markers
Scissors
Glue

Making the Elephant Toss

1. Decorate a clean, empty coffee can to look like an elephant's face. Cover the can with gray construction paper. Copy the pattern on gray construction paper. Glue on the face, ears, and trunk as shown.
2. To play the game, place your elephant on the ground. Have children stand three or four feet back from it. Each player gets three peanuts and the chance to throw them one at a time in the can to feed the elephant.
3. Allow every player to win a prize. For players that score, award them a small bag of peanuts!

Shepherd Name Card

King David wrote the twenty-third Psalm. In this Psalm, the king tells how God loves us and takes care of us like a Shepherd.

Bible Verse

The LORD is my Shepherd, I shall not be in want. Psalm 23:1

Materials Needed

Duplicated pattern on page 57
Typing paper
Poster board
Candy cane

Tools to Use

Markers and crayons
Scissors
Tape
Glue

Making the Shepherd Name Card

1. Duplicate the pattern on white paper. Color the shepherd and cut it out. Write a guest's name on the blank to put at each place setting.
2. Cut the poster board into a 5" x 16½" piece. Fold the poster board in half and fold over one inch from each end. Using the illustration as a guide, overlap the bottom folds and glue in place to form the base of the name card, using tape as needed.
3. Glue the shepherd to the front of the poster board. Tape a candy cane in the shepherd's hand to resemble a shepherd's staff.
4. Put a name card at each place setting around your table.

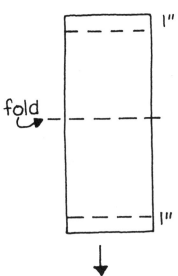

King David's Crown

King David knew about the goodness of God. As we decorate our crowns and nibble on the treats, think about the good things God gives to us.

Bible Verse

Taste and see that the LORD is good; blessed is the man who takes refuge in Him. Psalm 34:8

Materials Needed

Duplicated crown pattern from page 58

Yellow or gold poster board

White batting, suitable for making quilts, cut into 2′ × 1″ strips

Small red jawbreakers

Tools to Use

Scissors
Pencil
Glue stick

Making the Crown

1. Trace the crown pattern onto the poster board and cut out the crown.
2. Measure the crown to fit the child's head, adding two extra inches for gluing the ends together.
3. Spread the crown out flat on a work surface.
4. Glue the white batting along the bottom edge of the crown, trimming as needed.
5. Glue the wrapped candy on the crown as jewels.
6. Form a circle and glue or staple the ends of the crown together.
7. Carefully spread a line of glue around the bottom edge of the inside of the crown.
8. Wear when dry.

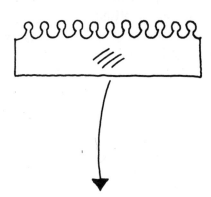

batting

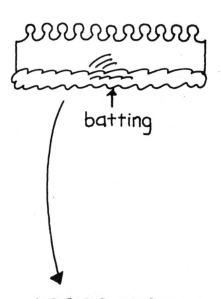

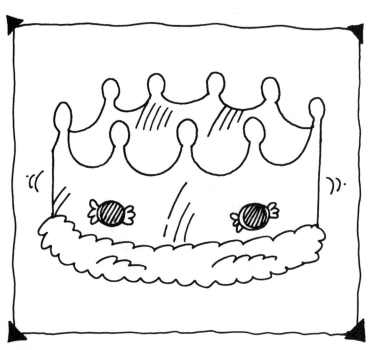

Marshmallow Spear

Reading the Bible can be as sweet and fun as eating something scrumptious!

Bible Verse

How sweet are Your words to my taste, sweeter than honey to my mouth!
Psalm 119:103

Materials Needed

Large marshmallow
10" long candy-filled straw or pretzel sticks
Chocolate suitable for melting
Candy sprinkles

Tools to Use

Bowl or pan
Spoon to stir chocolate

Making the Marshmallow Spear

1. Melt the chocolate in a pan on the stove or in a microwave.
2. Spear the marshmallow onto the end of the candy-filled straw or pretzel.
3. Dip the marshmallow into the melted chocolate, coating it three-fourths of the way along its sides. Roll this in sprinkles for a sweet and tasty treat.

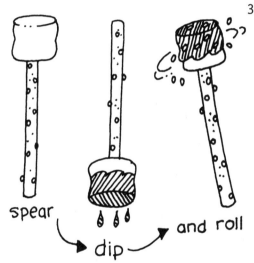

spear → dip → and roll

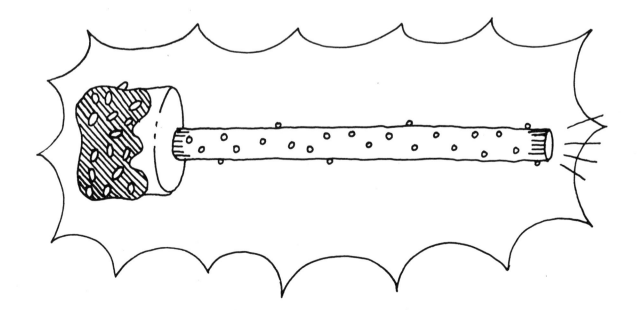

Uniquely You Accessory

God knows each one of us. He created us to be individuals with our own unique personalities. An accessory is something we wear. As we make this accessory and decide how to wear it, we can celebrate the fact that God loves each of us because He made us.

Bible Verse

O Lord, You have searched me and You know me. You know when I sit and when I rise; You perceive my thoughts from afar. Psalm 139:1–2

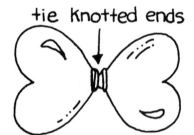

Materials Needed

Two 7" heart balloons
One long animal balloon
Ribbon suitable for curling
Variety of stick-shaped candy such as:
  Candy-filled straws
  Licorice sticks

Tools to Use

Small air pump, optional
Scissors

Making the Uniquely You Accessory

1. Inflate the heart balloons and knot their ends. Tie them together at the knotted ends.
2. Inflate three inches of air into the end of the long animal balloon and knot.
3. Using the inflated end of the balloon as a decorative front for the accessory, wrap the animal balloon once around the knotted center of the heart balloons. Tie the knotted end of the animal balloon to the beginning of the uninflated area.
4. Form a circle with the uninflated animal balloon and tie the end to the previous knot.
5. Stick two or three pieces of stick-shaped candy horizontally through the center inflated front of the accessory.
6. Decorate freely with ribbons, curling as desired.
7. Older children may wear the accessory as a hairbow, a bowtie, a wristband, or however they uniquely decide!

BOW OF BEAUTY

Proverbs 31 describes a beautiful woman as someone who loves God and her family.

Bible Verse

Charm is deceptive, and beauty is fleeting; but a woman who fears the LORD is to be praised.
Proverbs 31:30

Materials Needed

Clear vinyl, found in fabric stores
Back of a barrette
Narrow ribbon (curling ribbon works fine)
Assortment of small gum balls

Tools to Use

Hole punch
Scissors

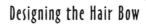

Designing the Hair Bow

1. Cut a 6" square of vinyl.
2. Fold the vinyl in half and punch holes all around the open edge, not the folded edge. Space the holes ½" apart, being careful not to get too close to the edge.
3. Match up the holes and keep them aligned. Begin at one corner of the vinyl and tie a 4' length of ribbon through the hole. Make a knot. Be careful not to tug too hard while you are making the knot since this will rip the vinyl.
4. Thread the ribbon through all the holes around the two edges of the vinyl.
5. Place about 20 gumballs into the vinyl pocket and finish sewing the vinyl closed. Tie a knot at the corner and trim off the ends of the ribbon.
6. Squish the vinyl gently in the center to form the shape of the hair bow, making sure that half the gum balls are on either end of the bow. Use a 32" length of ribbon to tie the barrette backing tightly to the center of the hair bow. Knot the ribbon in the front and form a decorative bow from the ribbon.

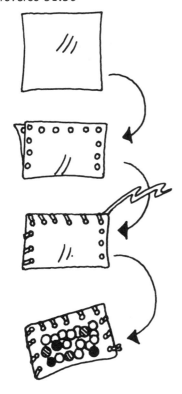

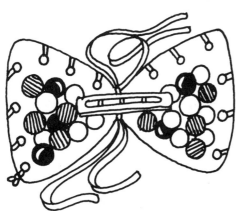

back view

front view

Happiness Necklaces

Today can be a time to laugh and dance because it is a day that the Lord has made. To help us feel happy, we can design our very own necklaces to wear and eat!

Bible Verse

[There is] a time to weep and a time to laugh, a time to mourn and a time to dance. Ecclesiastes 3:4

Shiny Necklace

Materials Needed

4' lengths of plastic wrap
Variety of round candy such as:
 Malt balls
 Gum balls
 Sour balls
Ribbon cut into 8" pieces

Tools to Use

Scissors

Making the Shiny Necklace

1. Spread the plastic wrap out flat on a table.
2. Place the candy along one long edge of the plastic wrap, spacing each piece of candy two or three inches apart.
3. Beginning at the edge with the candy, roll up the plastic wrap. Squeeze between each piece of candy to prevent sliding. When finished, the project will resemble a long, thin rope.
4. Tie a piece of ribbon tightly between each candy.
5. Tie the ends of the necklace together and wear.

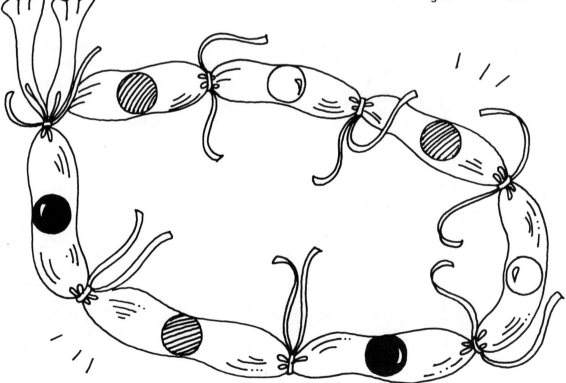

Scrumptious Necklace

Materials Needed

- 4' lengths of thin fabric ribbon
- Variety of candy that has a hole, including licorice or round candy
- Variety of cereal that has a hole in the middle of each piece

Tools to Use

Scissors

Making the Scrumptious Necklace

1. String the candy and cereal on the ribbon. It may help to tie a candy towards one end. A 2" length of ribbon should be left on the end for tying.
2. Tie the ends of the ribbon together to finish the necklace.

Strawberry Flower Centerpiece

During a wedding or other celebration, flowers can be used as decorations to help us remember God, who created every beautiful thing.

Bible Verse

Flowers appear on the earth; the season of singing has come.
Song of Songs 2:12

Materials Needed

One dozen whole, fresh strawberries
Firm head of lettuce
One dozen 10" bamboo skewers as found in the barbecue section of the grocery store
Basket the same size as the head of lettuce
Plastic wrap

Making the Strawberry Flower Centerpiece

1. Line the basket with plastic wrap.
2. Place the head of lettuce in the basket, fluffing out the leaves as much as possible. Put the core of the lettuce at the bottom of the basket.
3. Wash and dry each strawberry. Stick one strawberry on the end of each skewer so that the bottom tip of the strawberry points up.
4. Push the other end of the skewer into the head of lettuce.
5. Put the remaining strawberries on the skewers and stick the skewers into the lettuce to resemble a flower arrangement.
6. Use this centerpiece to decorate your table.

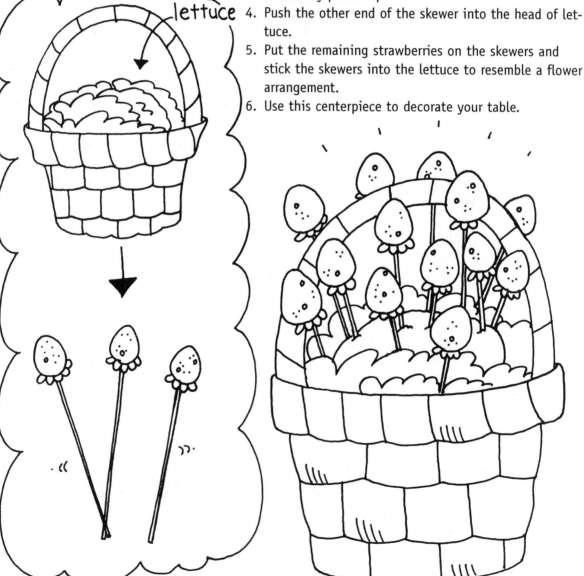

Star Glasses

When the Wise Men searched for Jesus, a star led them to His house. They were joyful when they found the newborn King. We, too, can celebrate with joy as we remember this important time.

Bible Verse

When they saw the star, they were overjoyed.
Matthew 2:10

Materials Needed

Duplicated glasses pattern as found on page 57
Poster board
Clear cellophane
Various colors of ribbon suitable for curling
Foil star stickers
Variety of individually wrapped candy such as:
   hard candy
   peppermints

Tools to Use

Glue stick
Scissors
Hole punch

Making the Star Glasses

1. Trace the star glasses pattern onto a piece of folded poster board and cut out.
2. Using the glasses pattern as a guide, cut out two pieces of cellophane large enough to use as lenses.
3. Glue the cellophane to the inside of the glasses.
4. Punch a hole at each temple and tie on 2' lengths of ribbon. Curl the ribbon.
5. Decorate the glasses with foil star stickers.
6. Glue wrapped candy at random on the front of the glasses or punch a hole in the wrappers and tie the candy to the ends of the ribbon pieces.

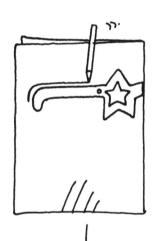

Decorated Spoon

Jesus explained to us that we don't need to worry about anything. God will take care of us. As we use our spoon and the bookmark that goes with it, let's tell our worries to God and trust in His help.

Bible Verse

"And why do you worry about clothes? See how the lilies of the field grow. They do not labor or spin." Matthew 6:28

Materials Needed

Duplicated pattern from page 56
Felt in assorted colors, including green
Plastic spoon
Round, candy-filled lollipop
Ribbon suitable for curling

Tools to Use

Craft glue suitable for felt
Scissors

Making the Spoon

1. Use the pattern to cut three pieces of felt into a green flower stem, a flower center and petals in contrasting colors.
2. Make the bookmark by gluing the center on the petals and gluing the stem on the back of the flower as shown.
3. Place the lollipop on the concave side of the spoon. Place the flower on the other side of the spoon. Tie all three items together with ribbon, curling the ends.
4. This spoon may be placed at a place setting.

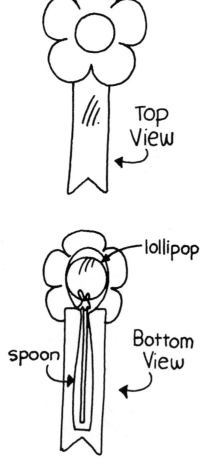

Sheep Puppet Treats

Jesus taught His followers that one day God would separate the bad people from the good people just as a shepherd separates the goats from the sheep. Jesus said that all who believe in Him as their Savior from sin and share God's love by acting kindly toward others would be like the sheep and would live in heaven forever.

Bible Verse

"The King will reply, 'I tell you the truth, whatever you did for one of the least of these brothers of Mine, you did for Me.'" Matthew 25:40

Materials Needed

Duplicated patterns from pages 59
Solid colored lunch-sized paper bag
Assortment of wrapped candy and other party favors such as:
  Small bag of popcorn
  Small toys

Tools to Use

Scissors
Crayons or markers
Stapler

Making the Sheep Puppet Treats

1. Cut out the pattern of the sheep and color.
2. Glue the top of the sheep's face to the bottom fold of the bag. Glue the bottom of the face under the fold of the bag.
3. Fill the bag with treats and staple the bottom shut.
4. Set the treat bag at each person's place setting. To eat the treats, cut off the bottom of the bag or remove the staples. When empty, use the bag as a puppet.

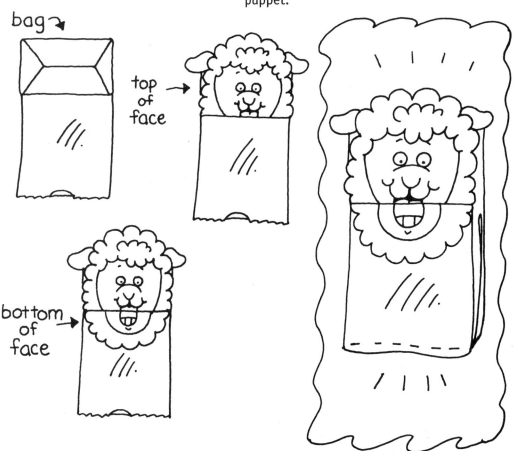

Chew-Chew Train

When parents brought their children to Jesus, the disciples told them to go away. Jesus scolded the disciples and let the little children come to Him. He held the children in His arms and blessed them. We can use this edible toy to give to children we know. As they play with it and eat it, we can tell them that Jesus loves them.

Bible Verse

When Jesus saw this, He was indignant. He said to them, "Let the little children come to Me, and do not hinder them, for the kingdom of God belongs to such as these." Mark 10:14

Materials Needed

Wrapped hard candies in these shapes:
   One small square
   One small cylinder
   One long cylinder
   Four flat circles
Use illustration as a guide.

Tools to Use

Hot glue gun

Making the Train

1. Follow the illustration as a guide to glue the square and small cylinder on top of the long cylinder.
2. Glue on the four flat circles as wheels.

WELCOME WREATH

One of the Pharisees invited Jesus to eat dinner with Him, but the Pharisee didn't wash Jesus' feet. That meant that he did not make Him feel welcome. When a woman arrived and washed Jesus' feet with her hair and expensive perfume, Jesus explained that she wasn't just washing His feet, she was showing her love for Him. As your guests arrive, greet them with the treats on this wreath to make them feel welcome.

Bible Verse

Then He turned toward the woman and said to Simon, "Do you see this woman? I came into your house. You did not give Me any water for My feet, but she wet My feet with her tears and wiped them with her hair." Luke 7:44

Materials Needed

Large wreath, such as an artificial evergreen
Ribbon suitable for curling
Fabric netting
Assorted candy

Tools to Use

Scissors

Decorating the Welcome Wreath

1. Cut the netting into 6" or 10" squares, depending on the size of your wreath and the number of your guests.
2. Place an assortment of candy in the center of each square of netting and tie into a parcel. Curl the ribbon.
3. Tie the net parcels at random onto the wreath, using the ribbon.
4. Hang the wreath in an entry. As your friends arrive, cut off the net parcels and welcome each person with a gift of candy.

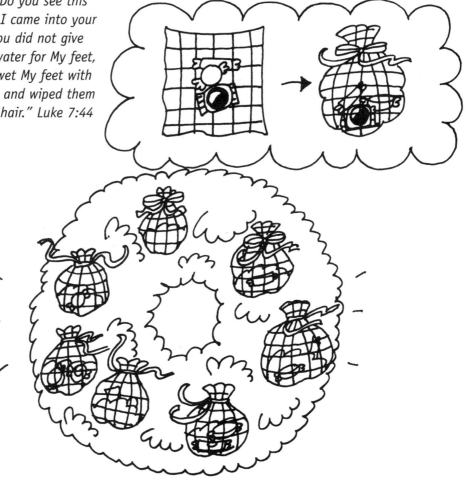

Birds' Nests

Jesus tried to explain to His disciples about the things they would need to do if they wanted to follow Him. Jesus did not want them to make up excuses. He wanted people to follow Him with all their hearts.

Bible Verse

Jesus replied, "Foxes have holes and birds of the air have nests, but the Son of Man has no place to lay His head." Luke 9:58

Materials Needed

Crispy rice cereal, six cups
¼ stick of butter or margarine
Marshmallows, one 10 oz. bag
Green food coloring
Jelly beans in a variety of colors

Tools to Use

Wooden spoon
Large pan
Nonstick muffin tins

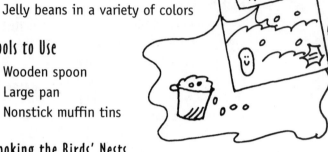

Cooking the Birds' Nests

1. Melt ¼ stick of butter or margarine in a large pan on the stove. Add the marshmallows, and stir them with a wooden spoon until melted. Stir in enough food coloring to make the mixture green.
2. Stir in six cups of crispy rice cereal.
3. Butter your fingers and press handfuls of the coated cereal into the muffin tins, making an indentation in the center of each to resemble a nest.
4. When cool and hard, remove the nests from the muffin tins. Put a handful of jelly bean eggs inside each nest to serve.

Mary and Martha Treats

Two sisters invited Jesus to visit their home. As Martha cooked and cleaned and worked, she became upset that her sister Mary simply sat at Jesus' feet and listened to Him talk. When Martha complained about this to Jesus, Jesus explained that it was all right for Mary to sit and listen to His words.

Bible Verse

"Martha, Martha," the Lord answered, "you are worried and upset about many things, but only one thing is needed. Mary has chosen what is better, and it will not be taken away from her."
Luke 10:41–42

Materials Needed

Duplicated patterns on page 60
Clear, plastic vinyl as found in craft stores, or lamination scraps
Large cookie cutters
Assortment of miniature candies

Tools to Use

Scissors
Embroidery needle
Heavy thread
Permanent marker
Clear tape

Making Mary and Martha Treats

1. Use the permanent marker to trace the cookie cutter or provided patterns onto a piece of clear vinyl. Repeat this procedure to make two pieces that match.
2. Cut out the two matching pieces. Gently fold one of the pieces and cut a 1" slit in the center of it. Put clear tape over this slit.
3. Use the needle and thread to sew the two pieces together, leaving a ¼" edge all around the shape. After sewing three-fourths of the way around the shape, put a dozen miniature candies in the clear pocket. Finish sewing.
4. Invite a friend over for a fun time of reading Bible stories. Give the treat you have made to your friend, and enjoy eating the sweets while listening to stories about Jesus, just as Mary did. To take out the candy, remove the tape from the slit.

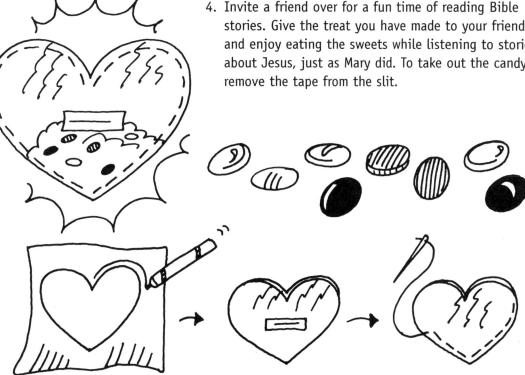

The Banquet's Garland

Jesus told His followers a parable about a man who invited many guests to his banquet. In the story, however, none of his guests came to the banquet. So the man invited poor people and everyone else he could think of to come and enjoy the feast. Jesus used this parable to show us that everyone is invited to become a Christian and live forever with Jesus in heaven.

Bible Verse

When one of those at the table with Him heard this, he said to Jesus, "Blessed is the man who will eat at the feast in the kingdom of God." Luke 14:15

Materials Needed

Strips of tinsel, 3-4' long
Fabric netting
Curling ribbon
Assortment of small wrapped candies
Small slips of paper with Bible verse printed on it

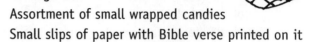

Tools to Use

Scissors

Making the Banquet's Garland

1. Cut the netting into 6" squares. Place an assortment of candies in the center of each square. Add the Bible verse. Gather up the edges and use curling ribbon to tie them together, forming small parcels.
2. Use curling ribbon to tie each parcel along the length of tinsel at 12" intervals.
3. Hang the garland around the room using pushpins or double-sided tape to attach each parcel to the wall or table. The tinsel will hang down in between each net parcel.
4. When the feasting is done, pass out the candy parcels to your guests.

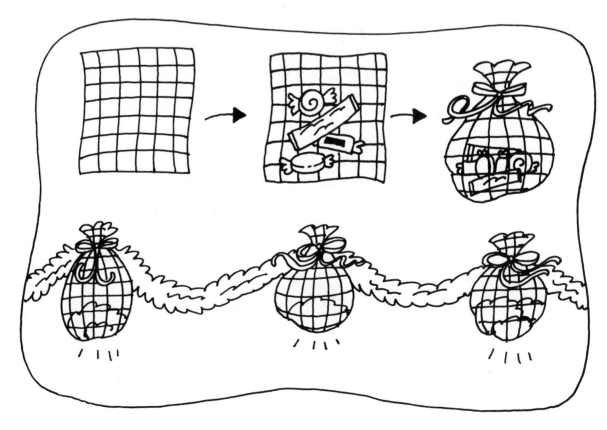

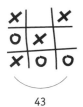

Search for the Lost Coin

Jesus compared the joy God has when someone becomes a Christian to the joy a woman might have if she finds a valuable coin she had lost.

Bible Verse

"In the same way, I tell you, there is rejoicing in the presence of the angels of God over one sinner who repents." Luke 15:10

Materials Needed

Gold foil-covered candy coins
Flashlights

Playing Search for the Lost Coin

1. To play this game, hide individual candy coins all around the room. Try to keep them visible, yet place them in out-of-the-way places. Hide enough coins for each player to find one.
2. When ready to play, read the parable of the lost coin aloud from Luke 15:8–10. Turn off the lights and give each player a flashlight, instructing them to find only one coin each.
3. After all the coins are found, turn on the lights. Encourage the children to share how excited they were when they found the coins. Compare this to the joy God feels when someone becomes a Christian.

44

Feeding the 5,000 Picnic Games

When Jesus performed a miracle and fed the 5,000 with five loaves of bread and two fish, the people began to realize who Jesus really was. What a picnic they had! Next time you have a picnic, say a prayer thanking God for sending His Son. Then play these games as you rejoice in the life God has given you.

Bible Verse

After the people saw the miraculous sign that Jesus did, they began to say, "Surely this is the Prophet who is to come into the world."
John 6:14

Bubble Gum Contest

Materials Needed

Large stick of bubble gum for each player

Tools to Use

Duplicated copy of instructions from page 61
Curling ribbon
Scissors
Whistle

Making the Bubble Gum

1. Use the curling ribbon to tie a duplicated copy of the playing instructions onto the large piece of gum.

Playing the Bubble Gum Contest

1. Give each player a piece of wrapped gum.
2. When the leader blows the whistle, all the players put the gum into their mouths and begin to chew.
3. When the leader blows the whistle again, all the players try to blow the biggest bubble.
4. Judges decide who wins.

Waffle Cone Toss

Materials Needed
Waffle cones
Large marshmallows

Tools to Use
None

Playing the Game

1. Divide the players into pairs. Each pair gets two cones and one marshmallow.
2. Stand the players in two long lines with the players facing their partners, about three feet apart.
3. Have the players in one line hold the marshmallow in their cones. On the count of three, have the players in this line throw the marshmallow from their cone to their partner's. Their partners should try to catch the marshmallows in their cones.
4. Players who drop their marshmallows are out. Players who catch their marshmallows continue the game.
5. Continue the game by having one line take one giant step backward. The last pair of players to catch the marshmallow wins the game.

Marshmallow Tag

Materials Needed
Large marshmallows

Tools to Use
None

Playing Marshmallow Tag

1. Give each player three large marshmallows. Explain that each player will try to tag someone by throwing a marshmallow and hitting another person with it. (Note: For safety, tell the children to aim below the neck.)
2. When someone is hit by a marshmallow, that player must sit down. The last person still standing wins the game. Players may pick up marshmallows from the ground for throwing.

Dramatic Masks

When Lazarus died, Jesus raised him from the dead. This helped many people believe that Jesus was actually the Son of God. Today, after creating our own unique masks, we can act out this story for others to see and also believe.

Bible Verse

Jesus said to her, "I am the resurrection and the life. He who believes in Me will live, even though he dies; and whoever lives and believes in Me will never die. Do you believe this?"
John 11:25–26

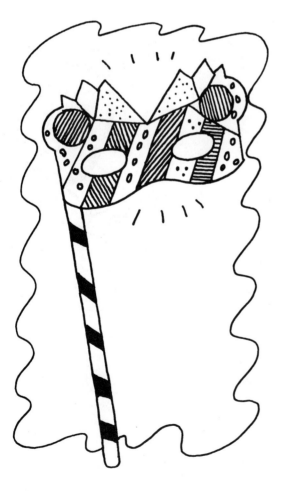

Materials Needed

Duplicated mask pattern from page 61
Poster board
Jumbo candy-filled straw, about 2' long
Cookie sprinkles in a variety of textures and colors
Small candies such as jelly beans

Tools to Use

Glue stick
Scissors
Pencils
Cake pans, one for each color of cookie sprinkles
Stapler
Clear tape

Designing the Dramatic Mask

1. Trace the mask pattern onto poster board and cut it out.
2. Draw a simple design on the front of the mask using diamonds, stripes, or circles.
3. Determine the color you want each space to be. Spread glue on all the spaces that will be decorated in the same color. Holding the mask over a cake pan, sprinkle the desired color of sprinkles on the areas covered with glue. Tilt the mask to pour any excess sprinkles into the cake pan. The extra can then be used by someone else.
4. Repeat with more glue and cookie sprinkles until all parts of the mask are decorated. Add jelly beans as desired.
5. Carefully spread a line of glue along the inside edge of the mask. Glue a candy-filled straw to the mask to form a handle. Staple if necessary. Cover the staple ends with clear tape to prevent scratching.
6. Give everyone a part to perform in the play. The cast can include Mary, Martha, Lazarus, Jesus, the disciples, and the mourners. Using John 11:1–44 as a guide, wear the masks to perform.
7. After the play is finished, offer the children the opportunity to proclaim their belief in Jesus as the Son of God.

The Servant's Sandals

Jesus taught His disciples to be servants to each other and to show God's love. At the Last Supper, the disciples took off their sandals and Jesus washed their feet. We can follow Jesus' example of being a servant by helping others and by doing kind things.

Bible Verse

"I have set you an example that you should do as I have done for you." John 13:15

Materials Needed

Two peanut-shaped cookies
Bubble gum strips
Prepared frosting
Small plastic bags
Ribbon

Tools to Use

Plastic knife
Scissors
Pen or pencil

Making the Servant's Sandals

1. Use scissors to cut the gum into ½" × 1 ½" strips. These will be the straps on the sandals.
2. Use the knife to place a spot of frosting on the sides of the cookie where the sandal straps will be attached. This will be the "glue" that holds the straps on the cookie.
3. Put the straps on the cookie as shown.
4. Fill out a card by writing down one kind thing you can do for someone you know. These could be kind things like making your bed, folding your laundry, helping with the dishes, or telling a story.
5. Put a pair of Servant's Sandals inside a bag. Tie the bag closed and attach the card. Give the sandals as a gift to someone, then serve your friend as Jesus taught us.

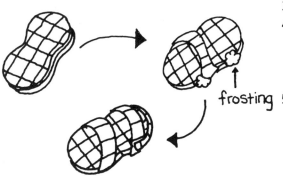

Resurrection Celebration

On the first Easter morning, the women and the disciples found an empty tomb. An angel appeared and told them that Jesus had risen from the dead.

Bible Verse

He is not here; He has risen! Luke 24:6a

Materials Needed

Empty egg carton
Plastic Easter eggs, one dozen
Sugar cookies, already baked but not decorated
Small paintbrush
Frosting
Food colors

Tools to Use

Paper cups
Plastic spoons

Having the Resurrection Celebration

1. Divide the frosting into the paper cups. Make different colors of frosting by stirring food coloring into each cup.
2. Open the plastic eggs, and put the bottom section of each egg in the egg carton.
3. Scoop several spoonfuls of frosting into each egg bottom, using one color per egg.
4. Put the tops on each egg for storage so the frosting does not dry out.
5. Use the paintbrush to 'paint' the frosting on the cookies—and celebrate! Jesus is alive!

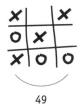

Bingo Love!

In his letter to the Corinthians, the apostle Paul teaches us the importance of love.

Bible Verse

And now these three remain: faith, hope and love. But the greatest of these is love.
1 Corinthians 13:13

Materials Needed

Duplicated patterns from pages 62-63
Bag to hold the set of bingo numbers
Small valentine candy hearts

Tools to Use

Scissors
Crayons or markers

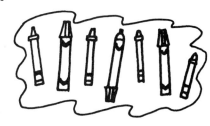

Making the Bingo Game

1. Duplicate the pattern for the bingo cards and cut out the cards. If more than six children will be playing bingo, duplicate the blank card for the correct number of players. Write numbers at random in the squares on the cards. Make small corresponding numbers to use for calling each number.
2. Color the bingo cards, if desired.
3. Give each player a handful of candy to use as markers.
4. Place all the bingo numbers into a bag. Pick one number out of the bag at a time, calling this number out loud. Players cover the number with a candy, if it is on their card. The winner is the first player to cover all the numbers in a row.

Fruit of the Spirit Bracelet

As we learn more about Jesus and God, it is important that our faith show itself in good qualities. These good things are described in the Bible as fruit of the Spirit. To help us remember the kinds of fruit the Holy Spirit grows in our lives, we can wear our bracelets. After the bracelets have been eaten, we can read the bookmark.

Bible Verse

But the fruit of the Spirit is love, joy, peace, patience, kindness, goodness, faithfulness, gentleness and self-control. Against such things is no law.
Galatians 5:22-23

Materials Needed

12" lengths of thin fabric ribbon
Hard candy with a hole in the center
Soft candy with a hole
Cereal with a hole
Duplicated pattern of the bookmark on page 64
Clear adhesive paper

Tools to Use

Scissors
Crayons or markers

Making the Fruit of the Spirit Bracelet

1. String the candy and cereal on the ribbon.
2. Fit the bracelet around your wrist and tie the ends of the ribbon together. Ask a friend to help you.
3. Practice reciting the Bible verse as you wear the bracelet. Beginning at one end and working toward the other, point to a different candy or cereal each time you say a different fruit of the Spirit.

Making the Bookmark

1. Cut out the bookmarks and color them.
2. Cover the bookmarks with clear adhesive paper or laminate.

ANCHOR OF HOPE BALLOON

God promised Abraham He would bless him. As Christians, we can believe God will keep His promises.

Bible Verse

We have this hope as an anchor for the soul, firm and secure.
Hebrews 6:19

Materials Needed

Balloon, filled with helium
Curling ribbon, various colors
Small box of candy
Gift wrap

Tools to Use

Scissors
Tape

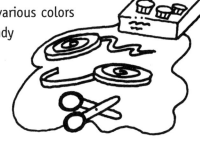

Making the Anchor of Hope Balloon

1. Wrap the box of candy with gift wrap.
2. Tie ribbon around the box.
3. Tie a 4′ length of ribbon to the balloon and tie it to the box of candy as an anchor. Anchor the balloon on each person's chair as a party favor or in the center of the table as a decoration to take home.

52 (BALLOON CLOWN PATTERN

BEE BASKET PATTERN) 53

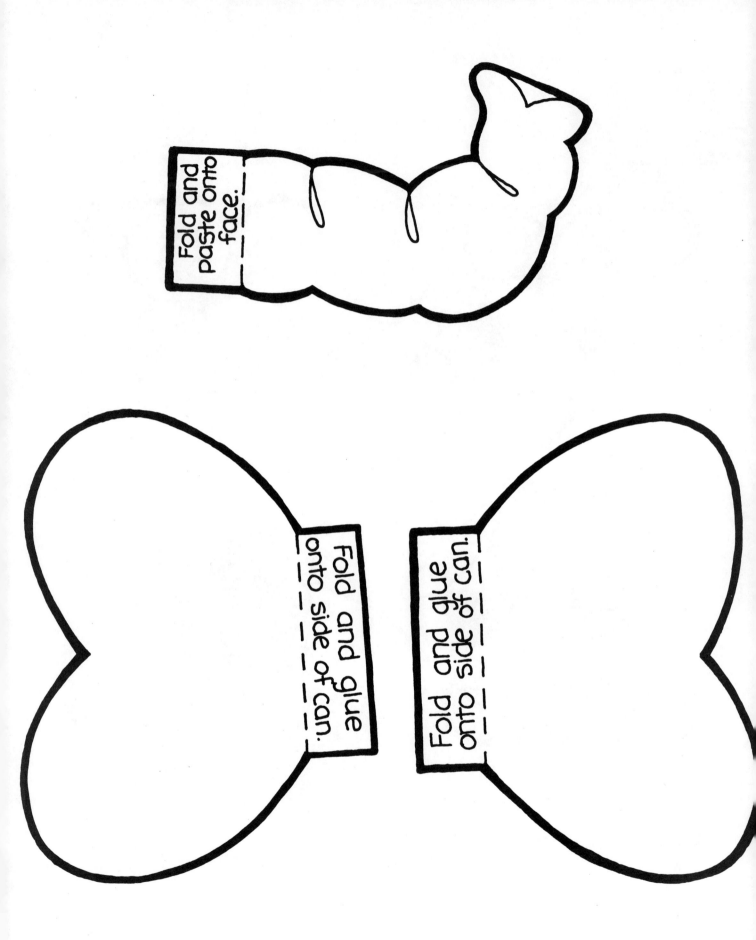

54 (ELEPHANT TOSS PATTERN

ELEPHANT TOSS PATTERN) 55

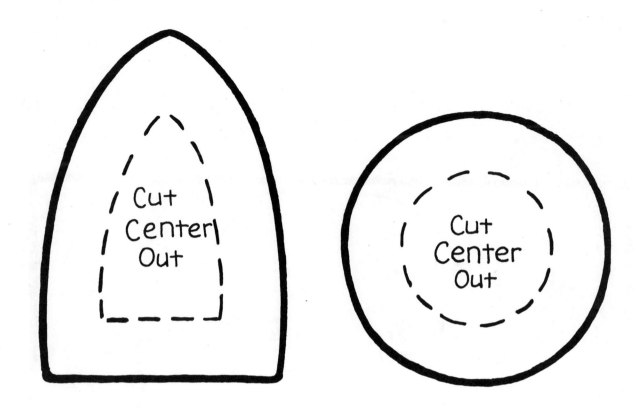

(STAINED-GLASS COOKIES PATTERN

56 (DECORATED SPOON PATTERN

(SHEPHERD NAME CARD PATTERN

STAR GLASSES PATTERN) 57

Place on Fold

Include two inches
more on each end
to allow for sizing.

58 (KING DAVID'S CROWN PATTERN

SHEEP PUPPET TREATS PATTERN) 59

60 (MARY AND MARTHA TREATS PATTERN

(BUBBLE GUM CONTEST PLAYING INSTRUCTIONS

DRAMATIC MASKS PATTERN) 61

♡	L	O	V	E
♡1	L1	O1	V1	E1
♡2	L2	O2	V2	E2
♡3	L3	O3	V3	E3
♡4	L4	O4	V4	E4
♡5	L5	O5	V5	E5
♡6	L6	O6	V6	E6
♡7	L7	O7	V7	E7
♡8	L8	O8	V8	E8
♡9	L9	O9	V9	E9
♡10	L10	O10	V10	E10
♡11	L11	O11	V11	E11
♡12	L12	O12	V12	E12
♡13	L13	O13	V13	E13
♡14	L14	O14	V14	E14
♡15	L15	O15	V15	E15
♡16	L16	O16	V16	E16
♡17	L17	O17	V17	E17
♡18	L18	O18	V18	E18
♡19	L19	O19	V19	E19
♡20	L20	O20	V20	E20

♡ L O V E

♡
Free Space

♡ L O V E

♡
Free Space

♡ L O V E

♡
Free Space

♡ L O V E

♡
Free Space

But the fruit of the Spirit is:

 LOVE

 JOY

 PEACE

 PATIENCE

 KINDNESS

 GOODNESS

 FAITHFULNESS

 GENTLENESS

 SELF-CONTROL

Against such things there is no law.
Galatians 5:22-23

But the fruit of the Spirit is:

 LOVE

 JOY

 PEACE

 PATIENCE

 KINDNESS

 GOODNESS

 FAITHFULNESS

 GENTLENESS

 SELF-CONTROL

Against such things there is no law.
Galatians 5:22-23

(FRUIT OF THE SPIRIT BOOKMARKS